ANNEMARIE ROSIER

EVERYDAY
MICROWAVE
COOKERY

A THORPAC COOKBOOK

A Martin Book

Published by Martin Books
An imprint of Woodhead-Faulkner Limited
Fitzwilliam House, 32 Trumpington Street
Cambridge CB2 1QY
in association with Thorpac Group plc
1 Elliot Road, Love Lane Industrial Estate
Cirencester, Glos GL7 1LU

First published 1984
Second impression 1985
© Thorpac Group plc 1984
ISBN 0 85941 217 2

Photography: John Lee
Cover design: Pentagram
Text design: Ron Jones
Typeset by Westholme Graphics Limited
Printed and bound in Great Britain by
Springbourne Press Limited, Basildon, Essex

Contents

Preface

The marvellously versatile microwave cooker is now a feature of many modern kitchens, but so many owners I encounter just do not realise the full cooking potential of their appliances. So often the cooker is just used for jacket potatoes, or to warm up pies! In *Everyday Microwave Cookery* I show how your microwave cooker can be used in all kinds of useful and unexpected ways in day-to-day meal-making, and also reveal to the practised microwave user many new ideas for use and a range of interesting recipes to add to your cooking repertoire. Once you start using your cooker in different ways, you will find that the possibilities are endless!

An important aspect often overlooked in microwave cookery is the appropriate use of cooking containers. Ever since Man formed his first clay cooking pot to use on an open fire, specific containers for cooking have been essential. Whether cooking by gas, electricity, solid fuel or microwave, you need the correct containers to achieve the best results. All the dishes used in this book are either from the Thorpac Durable Microwave Cookware Range or from the Thorpac Disposable Range. The Durable Range has been designed and made in Britain with our everyday cooking and eating habits in mind. All are suitable for the freezer and yet look very elegant on the table.

The recipes chosen for this book are simple to do and alternative ingredients have been suggested to give variety. Starred dishes are suitable for freezing and then defrosting and heating at a later time.

I would like to thank Philips Electronics and Toshiba UK Limited for the loan of their microwave cookers, in which my recipes were tested. I would also like to acknowledge the patience and co-operation of my night school class, family and friends in tasting the end results!

Annemarie Rosier

Introduction

The microwave cooker in your kitchen

Once you own a microwave cooker, it soon becomes an indispensable part of the family way of life. Like any piece of equipment, it takes a little time to get used to, so if you have a disaster with your first cake, just use it as a base of a trifle or turn it into a steamed microwave pudding and try again! Before long you will be producing all manner of snacks, main courses and delicious puddings to impress your family and friends.

Cooking with a microwave is cheap, since the microwave cooker uses very little electricity compared to a conventional oven. You will also find that you have less washing up, as food can often be served up in the cooking containers themselves. The kitchen remains cleaner and cooler during cooking, as a minimal amount of dirt, grease or steam is produced. Meal planning will become easier too, as prepared and frozen food can be quickly defrosted and heated up. Cooking just won't seem the same chore again!

Use your microwave cooker in conjunction with other kitchen equipment to create perfectly finished dishes every time. For instance, sometimes a crisped or browned effect is desired, and a grill can be used for the final few minutes of cooking. Use a frying pan to pre-colour meat for your casseroles, etc., and try using a conventional oven for part-cooking food such as roast potatoes. Toast or crumpets cooked in a toaster can be simply heated up in a microwave cooker. If you are using dried food such as pasta, rice or packet soups, boil the water in a kettle to save time before final cooking in the microwave.

The microwave cooker cannot cook all dishes well – Yorkshire puddings, soufflés, food in batter and boiled eggs are, for instance, some of its failures – and with some of your favourite recipes you may prefer the end results of a conventional cooker. But with imaginative use of your microwave and standard kitchen equipment there are very few dishes that cannot be achieved with perfect results every time.

The choice of microwave cooker

Over the last three years the domestic microwave market has extended dramatically and many different models are available. All perform the same basic functions – to defrost, cook and reheat food – but they incorporate various other features, which help both to extend the range of foods cooked and to improve on the end results.

The three basic types of microwave cooker

Counter Top Models	These can be placed on any suitable work surface and plugged into a 13 amp socket.
Double Oven Cookers	Part of a free-standing conventional oven, with the microwave being at eye level. OR In a double, built-in unit, where the microwave takes the place of a second, smaller oven.
Combination Cookers	These combine microwave and conventional cooking all in one oven. Usually the cooker is a counter top model. The microwave is generally operated separately or in sequence from the conventional heat.

Features of the microwave cooker

There are various features found in microwave cookers, such as variable power controls, temperature probes, turntables, touch control settings and different cavity sizes. It will depend on your individual family size and requirements as to which are the important microwave features for you. The two main features used in this cookbook are the Variable Power Control and the Temperature Probe.

Variable Power Control	This enables the oven to operate at different speeds. All cookers have two basic speeds, fast and slow, but a greater number of speeds allows more flexibility in cooking. (For example, if you can vary the power during cooking, casseroles and stews can be simmered gently, egg custards can be cooked without curdling and cakes can be cooked more evenly.) The slow is used mainly for defrosting. (Three settings have been used in this book – Full, Medium and Low – but these controls may be marked differently on your cooker, so see the chart on page 8 for comparative settings.)
Temperature Probe	This is a probe fitted into the cavity of the oven. The pointed end is inserted into the food, the required finishing temperature is set and the oven automatically switches off when the food reaches that temperature. It is useful for reheating, the cooking of joints, keeping foods warm and, in some cookers, simmering food over an extended period of time.

Variable Power setting chart

The cooker wattage used in this book is 650–720. Use this chart to find the approximate equivalent settings on your oven.

Cookbook settings	LOW	MEDIUM	FULL
Equivalent settings	Defrost Defrost 3 30	Medium Simmer 5 50	Full Power Cook 9 High

If your cooker has only two powers and a recipe in this book calls for a Medium setting, use the following chart as a guide for equivalent cooking times. For recipes where over 15 minutes cooking time is required, use Full Power.

Medium Setting in book (minutes)	Low Power (minutes)	Full Power (minutes)
2	3¼	1
4	7	2
6	10	3
8	13	4
10	17	5
12	20	6
14	23	7
16		8
18		9
20		10

Careful use of the microwave cooker

All forms of cooking have a few guide-lines to be remembered and this is especially important when using the microwave cooker. Read the owner's manual supplied with your microwave cooker for all the do's and don'ts in using the cooker, but remember the one big NO: do not place metal cooking containers in the cooker!

1 Stirring. If you stir liquids, e.g., casseroles, custards or baked beans, it helps the food to cook more evenly. Lumps in sauces are also avoided.

Thorpac Microwave Cookware (Disposable Range)

2 Prick or score.   Any food with a membrane or skin, such as eggs, kidneys and whole tomatoes, should be pricked or scored to prevent the food from bursting. Always prick Boilable Bags before using in the oven for defrosting and heating.

3 Standing time.   Food carries on cooking, heating or defrosting on removal from the oven, so this is an important part of the recipe and the timings given should be followed.

4 Timing of food.   All timings are approximate and depend on your oven and the starting temperature, age and preparation of the food. When following a recipe, therefore, under-time and then increase cooking time as necessary.

5 Number of portions.   The more food you place into the cooker the longer it will take to cook. For instance, one jacket potato takes approximately 6 minutes, but this time is increased for each additional potato by approximately 50–75%. Therefore two potatoes take 9 minutes, three take 12 minutes, and so on.

6 Placing of food.   The more evenly spaced the food is in the cooker the quicker and better it heats. Individual items should be placed in a circle, slightly separated. Thin ends of chops, poultry and fish should overlap or point towards the centre of the cooker.

7 Covering of food.   Cover dishes when defrosting, heating and cooking if you want the moisture to be kept in, i.e., for fish, vegetables and meat. Heat and cook uncovered when you want the foods to remain dry, i.e., with bread, cakes and pizza.

8 Turning of food.   Some large items of food cook better by being turned over once or twice during cooking. This mainly applies to poultry and joints of meat over 2 kg/5 lb.

9 Turning around.   If your cooker does not have a turntable, check with the manufacturer's instructions as to whether food should be turned round during cooking.

Microwave cookware

Even though metal cannot be used, many different materials are used in making microwave cookware. Some of these are only suitable for certain uses, others will cope with all cooking.

Materials suitable for microwave cooking are divided into two groups, disposable and durable.

Some Disposable Cookware and their uses

Paper Kitchen Towels	For absorbing moisture.
Paper Plates and Cups	For short reheating.
Plastic Foam Containers	For defrosting products, and reheating bread products.
Cling Film	For covering dishes without a lid.
Boilable Bags	For defrosting, cooking and heating. (Always prick before placing in the oven.)
Freezer Bags/Film	For defrosting only.
Roasting Bags	For covering joints and poultry during cooking.
Layering Tissue	For lining cake, loaf and flan dishes.
Plastics designed for use in the freezer	For some cooking, heating and defrosting. May distort with fats or sugar and discolour with some foods.

Durable containers

Any containers that are designed for the freezer and the dishwasher are usually suitable for the microwave, as long as they have a sealed or glazed surface and no gold or silver pattern.

It depends on the material as to how efficient the containers will be, as all have some ability to slow down the microwaves before they enter the food. It is generally recognised that the plastic UDEL Polysulfone has the lowest resistance to microwave energy. Being a plastic, UDEL Polysulfone is easy to mould and this is important, as the correct shape is essential for successful cooking. Microwaves can penetrate into food to a depth of 4 cm/1½ inches in all directions; therefore the perfect cooking shape is a ring no more than 7.5 cm/3 inches in depth or height. While this shape of container may be ideal for a limited number of cakes and puddings, it is not practical for casseroles, vegetables or sauces. So a compromise is made with round or oval shaped dishes.

Cookware should have rounded corners and edges, as tight or shaped corners can result in overcooking. It is also advisable to raise the dishes off the base of the oven with a small rim, to help even cooking. Contrary to popular belief, all dishes used in the microwave do not stay cold. Many materials absorb heat from the food where it touches the dish; so handles or rims are needed.

The successful container is therefore:

1 Low in resistance to microwave energy.
2 Rounded or oval in shape.
3 Slightly raised at the base.
4 Curved at the edges and corners.
5 Reasonably cool during cooking and with handles.
6 Also suitable for use in the freezer and dishwasher.
7 Suitable for use on the table as a serving dish.

These are all features of the Thorpac Range of microwave cookware.

Specialist cookware

All items mentioned here are from the Thorpac Durable Range and cover most cooking requirements. Just a few of the dishes' many uses are mentioned. All the cookware is chip and break resistant, resistant to staining and has easy-release properties.

Roasting Rack – Base and Rack	This is used for the cooking of meat and poultry so that they are not sitting in their own juices (see pages 72–73 for specific cooking instructions). Use also for the reheating of bread and pastry items.
Mini Dishes – 56.8 ml/ 2 fl oz single round dishes	These are used for poaching eggs and cooking individual puddings, pâtés and fairy cakes. Place in the cooker, arranged either in the Roasting Rack Base or in a circle to promote even cooking.
Shallow Dish – 1.2-litre/ 2-pint oval base and lid with temperature probe slot	The ideal dish for cooking fish, chops in sauce, lasagne, spare ribs and many other meals.

Thorpac Microwave Cookware (Durable Range)

Vegetable Dish – 1.2-litre/2-pint base and lid with temperature probe slot	Used for general vegetable cooking, milk puddings, casseroles for one or two persons and the reheating of canned foods.
Casserole Dish – large 2.3-litre/4-pint oval casserole and lid with temperature probe slot	This dish is large enough to take a family-size bacon joint, or 4 or more good chicken portions for a casserole, and is also useful for pasta and rice cooking.
Loaf Dish – 22 cm/ $8^5/8$-inch oblong, deep dish	A useful container for making terrines, wholemeal bread, cakes and meat loaves.
Cake Dish – 20 cm/ 8-inch round, deep cake dish	This dish has been domed slightly at the base to assist with the cooking of cakes. Use also for puddings.
Flan Dish – 20 cm/ 8-inch flan dish	Use for flans, open tarts, quiches and cheesecakes.

Jug – 1-litre/1¾-pint jug	With its rounded corners at the base, the Jug is perfect for sauces, custards, gravies and for assisting in the preparation of other dishes. Use also for scrambled eggs.

The following are from the Thorpac Disposable Range. Do not use for dishes with a high sugar or fat content.

900 g/2 lb Pudding Basin	For cooking, freezing and reheating. Use for Christmas puddings, steak and kidney puddings and for sponge puddings.
18 cm/7-inch Cake Dish	Use for cooking fruit, plain and fancy cakes, rice puddings and many other dishes.
17 cm/6¾-inch Pie Plate	Versatile for quiches, flans, tarts and many hot or cold, sweet or savoury dishes.

Also used in the book is a Browning Dish, readily available.

Cookware cleaning

Looking after the Microwave Cookware is simple. Both the Durable and Disposable Ranges can be washed in warm soapy water or placed in a dishwasher. Avoid using sharp instruments or wire wool as they will damage the surface. If any stains do occur, soak in a mild solution of tea or coffee pot cleaner. Rinse well before using.

Freezer to table

One of the joys of owning a microwave cooker is its ability to defrost and reheat without any alteration to the flavour, colour or moisture content of the food.

Defrosting is done on a lower power level than that generally used for cooking or heating. This helps the ice crystals to break down gently and evenly. It is important to ensure that food is completely thawed before heating and cooking, so do always stand food for the recommended times, as this is part of the defrosting cycle. The times for defrosting in the microwave cooker are very short compared to conventional thawing times: for example, 1.3 kg/3 lb chicken takes 20 minutes to defrost plus 20 minutes standing (compared to the conventional thawing time, which is overnight in the refrigerator). This allows for easier meal planning. Cooked food that is frozen at home will generally take longer to defrost than similar commercial varieties.

Many of the recipes cooked in this book can be frozen and reheated, and these are marked with a star (★). The food can be frozen in its cooking container or in a suitably sized Disposable Tray, Casserole Dish or Boilable Bag.

When packaging food for the freezer to defrost later, remember these points:

1 If *not* freezing in the cooking dish, use a similar size of container, so that the food is reasonably compact, i.e., meat balls do not protrude too much out of the sauce.

2 Ensure that the food is well chilled before covering and freezing.

3 Cover all trays with a suitable wrap or slide into a Freezer Bag. Seal or tie the Bag. Remember to undo the seal or tie when placing in the microwave cooker.

4 When freezing plated meals, ensure that all food is cooked. Raw food cannot be mixed with cooked on the same plate.

5 Label all food.

When defrosting food in the microwave cooker remember to:

1 Remove any ties or tags.

2 Loosen any tight coverings.

3 Break up casseroles, stews and soups as soon as possible, as this helps quicker and more even thawing.

4 Leave food loosely covered during standing.

Plated meals cooking chart

The microwave cooker can be used for the reheating of plated meals and puddings which have been frozen or refrigerated. Use the Thorpac Disposable Microwave Trays instead of plates in the freezer. Always defrost and reheat the food loosely covered.

Weight of plated meal	Defrost on Low (Defrost) Power	Reheat on Full Power
375 g/12 oz	3½–5 minutes	2–3 minutes
450 g/1 lb	5–7 minutes	3–4 minutes

Interesting uses for your microwave cooker

Every microwave user has his or her own favourite list of 'general jobs' for their cooker, and here are just a few ideas from microwave owners I have met!

Warming flour for bread making.
Softening butter for spreading on bread.
Heating honey or golden syrup for brushing on top of cakes.
Melting chocolate or marshmallows.
Softening hard brown sugar.
Softening dates for chopping.
Warming marzipan before rolling out.
Softening butter or margarine for cake making.
Blanching small amounts of vegetables before freezing.
Cooking chestnuts (make a slit in the skin).
Warming citrus fruit before squeezing, to give more juice.
Drying herbs.
Blanching potatoes for roasting or frying.
Boiling potato peelings for birds in the snow.
Drying breadcrumbs.
Warming sugar for jam making.
Heating babies' bottles and food.
Heating jam jars to remove that last tablespoon of jam.
Reheating cold coffee and tea.

Introduction to recipes

All the recipes in this book have been tested in a variety of microwave cookers, ranging from 650–720 watts. Three power levels have been used: Full, Medium and Low Power (see page 8 for the equivalent on your microwave cooker).

All timings are approximate, depending on the starting temperature, age, shape and preparation of the food. Microwave cookers also vary in speed, not only from manufacturer to manufacturer but also in individual models. Check your oven as you try a recipe for the first time and be prepared if necessary to allow more or less time in future. Cooking times do not include preparation.

All the dishes used in this book are from the Thorpac Durable and Disposable Ranges, except for the Browning Dish.

Note: If using a combination microwave cooker, do not place any of the dishes in the cooking cavity when it is hot or while the elements or warm air system are working.

Note on quantities
Ingredients in the recipes are given in both imperial and metric measures. Use either set, but not a mixture of both, in any one recipe. All spoon measurements are level unless otherwise stated.

Breakfast

Breakfast is a meal you love or hate and often the family is divided about what to have. The microwave cooker sorts out this problem and, since all the dishes are easy to do, children can often cook their own. Use these recipes for light meals or as part of a main meal.

Porridge

Cooking container : Casserole Dish
Cooking time : 7–8 minutes, plus 3 minutes standing time
Number of servings : 3–4

Ingredients:
50 g/2 oz porridge oats
300 ml/½ pint water
300 ml/½ pint milk
a good pinch of salt

Method:
Combine all the ingredients and put them in the Casserole Dish. Cover with the lid and cook for 7–8 minutes on Full Power. Stir once during cooking and on removal from the cooker. Stand for 3 minutes before serving.

Serve: topped with sugar and cream or extra salt.

Variation: for instant porridge/cereal, mix as instructed on the packet and then heat in a cereal bowl until boiling; 2–3 minutes on Full Power.

Sausages

Cooking container : Roasting Rack or Browning Dish
Cooking time : 12–14 minutes
Number of servings : 4–8

Ingredients:
450 g/1 lb thick sausages

Method:
Preheat the Browning Dish in the cooker for 6 minutes on Full Power. Separate the sausages and lightly prick the skins. Press the sausages on to the Dish; when coloured, turn over and cook for 6–8 minutes on Full Power, turning over every 3 minutes.

Serve: with own choice of breakfast.

Variation: cook the sausages for 6–8 minutes on the Roasting Rack and then brown under a grill or in a frying pan.

Kedgeree ★

Cooking containers : Mini Dishes/Shallow Dish
Cooking time : 14–16 minutes
Number of servings : 6 as a breakfast dish or 4 as a supper dish

Ingredients:
4 eggs (size 3)
350 g/12 oz smoked haddock, cooked
1 onion, chopped finely
50 g/2 oz butter
a good pinch of curry powder
175 g/6 oz rice, cooked
salt and pepper
chopped parsley, to garnish

Method:
Break the eggs into 4 Mini Dishes. Prick the yolks. Cook in the microwave for 4–6 minutes on Medium Power until the yolks are hard. Cut the eggs into quarters.

Remove the skin and bone from the fish and flake the fish meat. Cook the onion with the butter in the Shallow Dish, uncovered, for 4 minutes on Medium Power. Stir in the curry powder and then the rice. Mix well. Heat covered for 3 minutes on Full Power. Stir in the fish and egg, season, cover and heat for a further 3 minutes on Full Power.

Serve: garnished with the parsley.

Kedgeree; Kippers

Kippers

Cooking container	: Shallow Dish
Cooking time	: 7–9 minutes, plus 3–5 minutes standing time
Number of servings	: 4

Ingredients:
450 g/1 lb kippers, whole or filleted
40 g/1½ oz butter

Method:
Place the kippers in the Shallow Dish, overlapping the thinner edges, and dot with the butter. Cover the dish and cook for 7–9 minutes on Full Power. Stand covered for 3–5 minutes before serving.

Serve: with a lemon slice.

Variation: to serve one person, dot 150 g/5 oz fish with butter, cover and cook on Full Power for 2–3 minutes. Haddock and other fish can also be cooked in this way.

Poached Eggs

Cooking containers	: Mini Dishes/Roasting Rack Base (optional)
Cooking time	: 1¼–2 minutes, plus 1 minute standing time
Number of servings	: 4

Ingredients:
4 eggs (size 2)

Method:
Break the eggs into the Mini Dishes and prick the yolks of the eggs. Place in the Roasting Rack Base or form in a circle on the cooker tray. Cover with a piece of kitchen paper towelling. Cook on Full Power for 1¼–2 minutes. Stand for 1 minute or so before serving.

Serve: with brown bread or toast and butter.

Variation: for one egg, cook on Medium Power for 1–1¼

minutes. Instead of hard-boiling eggs, poach the eggs for a minute or so longer; then chop for sandwiches or use as required.

Milky Hot Drinks

Cooking container : Jug
Cooking time : See chart
Number of servings : 1–4

Ingredients:
For Coffee
milk
instant coffee
sugar, to taste

For Drinking Chocolate
milk
drinking chocolate powder
sugar, to taste

Method:
Heat the required amount of milk (see below) in the Jug on Full Power for the time suggested in the table. (Temperature Probe setting: 80°C/175°F.) Pour the milk into a cup or mug and stir in the coffee or chocolate. Sweeten to taste.

Cup 150 ml/¼ pint	Time
1	2 minutes
2	2–3 minutes
4	4–5 minutes

Mug 210 ml/7 fl oz	Time
1	2½ minutes
2	3–4 minutes
4	6–7 minutes

Variation: when heating milk for cereal the temperature required is less, so cut cup timings by a third. (Temperature Probe setting: 65–70°C/150–160°F.)

Bacon, Mushrooms and Tomatoes

Cooking container : Roasting Rack and Base
Cooking time   : 5–8 minutes
Number of servings : 4

Ingredients:
2 medium-size tomatoes
8 mushrooms
8 rashers of bacon

Method:
Cut the tomatoes in half and put in the Base of the Roasting Rack. Remove the stalks from the mushrooms and put the caps with the tomatoes. Snip the fat off the bacon and place on to the Rack, lapping fat over lean. Return the Rack to its Base. Cook in the microwave on Full Power for 5–8 minutes, depending on personal preference.

Serve: with poached eggs and toast or fried bread.

Eggs and Bacon

Cooking container : Browning Dish
Cooking time   : 9½–10½ minutes
Number of servings : 2

Ingredients:
4 rashers of back bacon
2 eggs (size 3)
2 tomatoes, sliced in halves

Method:
Heat the Browning Dish for 5 minutes on Full Power. Press the bacon and tomatoes on to the surface of the dish and cook for 2½ minutes on Full Power. Turn the bacon and tomatoes over and break the eggs into the dish; then prick the yolks. Cover the dish with its lid and cook for a further 2–3 minutes on Full Power, or until the eggs are cooked.

Serve: with toast for breakfast or with chips as a snack meal.

Croissants; Drinking Chocolate; Bacon, Poached Egg, Mushrooms and Tomatoes

Mixed Dried Fruit Salad

Cooking container : Vegetable Dish
Cooking time : 14 minutes, plus 30 minutes standing time
Number of servings : 4–5

Ingredients:
225 g/8 oz mixed dried fruit (e.g., apricots, prunes and apples)
600 ml/1 pint water
50 g/2 oz sugar

Method:
Place the dried fruit and the water in the Vegetable Dish and heat, covered, for 6 minutes on Full Power. Stir in the sugar and heat (still covered) for 8 minutes on Full Power. Allow to stand for 30 minutes to finish cooking. Chill before serving.

Serve: with cereal, milk or cream.

Variation: all dried fruit can be cooked this way.

Breakfast Bread Items

Cooking container : Roasting Rack
Cooking time : See chart
Number of servings : 1–4

Ingredients:
Fried bread, toast, croissants or bread rolls

Method:
All can be heated in the cooker. Place on the Roasting Rack, cover with kitchen paper towelling and heat on Full Power for the time shown.

Fried bread/toast
1 slice: 30 seconds
4 slices: 1¼–1½ minutes

Croissants/bread rolls
1: 15–20 seconds
4: 45–60 seconds

Light meals

These light meals are for anytime: lunch, when the children come home, as part of high tea or as late TV snacks. Many of the recipes can be cooked when you have the time, frozen down and then heated at 30 minutes notice. Also included is a re-heating chart for convenience foods.

Tomato-stuffed Peppers ★

Cooking containers : Casserole Dish/Shallow Dish
Cooking time   : 32–35 minutes
Number of servings : 4

Ingredients:
4 large green peppers
1 large onion, chopped
1 tablespoon oil
100 g/4 oz long grain rice
298 g/10½ oz can of condensed tomato soup
water
100 g/4 oz ham, chopped
6 small cocktail gherkins, chopped

Method:
Cut the tops off the peppers, putting them aside, and remove any seeds. Cook the onion in the oil, covered, in the Casserole Dish for 3 minutes on Medium Power. Stir in the rice and cook for a further 2 minutes on Medium Power. Stir in the tomato soup and 2 soup cans of water. Cook covered on Full Power for 12 minutes. Stir in the chopped ham and gherkins. Fill the peppers with the rice mixture. Place in the Shallow Dish, re-place the pepper tops and cover loosely with Cling Film or Layering Tissue. Cook for 15–18 minutes on Full Power or until the peppers are soft.

Serve: with toast and salad as a light meal or with mashed potatoes and additional vegetables as a main meal.

Variation: use cooked mincemeat mixed with rice or bread-crumbs as a stuffing.

Barbecued Spare Ribs ★

Cooking container : Shallow Dish
Cooking time : 25–30 minutes
Number of servings : 4

Ingredients:
550 g/1¼ lb spare ribs
15 g/½ oz butter
1 onion, chopped finely
2 cloves of garlic, crushed
110 ml/4 fl oz tomato ketchup
2 tablespoons wine vinegar
1 tablespoon tabasco sauce
4 tablespoons soft brown sugar

Method:
Seal and colour the spare ribs under a grill. Place into the Shallow Dish the butter, onion and garlic and cook covered on Medium Power for 5 minutes. Stir in the ketchup, vinegar, tabasco sauce and sugar. Place in the spare ribs and spoon over the sauce. Cook uncovered for 5 minutes on Full Power and then on Medium Power for 15–20 minutes until the ribs are tender.

Serve: with rice or noodles.

Cheese and Apple Open Toasties

Cooking container : Roasting Rack
Cooking time : 1½–2 minutes
Number of servings : 3

Ingredients:
100 g/4 oz cream cheese
50 g/2 oz Double Gloucester cheese, grated
3 thin slices of cooked ham
3 slices of wholemeal toast
1 large Cox's apple, cored and sliced thinly in rings
pickle
salt and pepper

Barbecued Spare Ribs with rice

Method:
Mix together the cream cheese and grated cheese; then season lightly. Place the ham on the toast, spread with the cream cheese and cover with the sliced apple rings. Place on to the Roasting Rack. Heat for 1½–2 minutes on Full Power.

Serve: topped with the pickle.

Variation: use salami or thinly sliced chicken instead of ham.

Lasagne ★

Cooking containers : Casserole Dish/Shallow Dish
Cooking time : 62–68 minutes
Number of servings : 4–5

Ingredients:
1.8 litres/3 pints boiling water
175 g/6 oz lasagne verdi
450 g/1 lb minced beef
100 g/4 oz green bacon
1 onion, chopped
1 stick of celery, chopped
1 carrot, chopped
397 g/14 oz can of tomatoes, chopped
50 g/2 oz butter
150 ml/¼ pint chicken stock
450 ml/¾ pint white sauce (see page 75)
175 g/6 oz cheese, grated
salt

Method:
Place the boiling water in the Casserole Dish with a little salt. Add the lasagne and cook, covered, for 12–15 minutes or until just tender, on Full Power. Drain the lasagne and lay the strips on kitchen paper towelling until required. Cook the mince and bacon in the Casserole Dish for 5 minutes on Full Power. Separate the meats and stir in the onion, celery and carrot; then cover and cook for 5 minutes on Full Power. Stir in the tomatoes, butter, chicken stock and a little salt. Cook covered

for 10 minutes on Full Power and then 20 minutes on Medium Power.

Place in the Shallow Dish half the meat sauce and cover with half the lasagne, half the white sauce and half the cheese. Repeat the layering. Heat, uncovered, for 10–13 minutes on Full Power or until hot.

Serve: with salad and french bread.

Macaroni Cheese ★

Cooking containers : Casserole Dish/Shallow Dish
Cooking time   : 27–30 minutes
Number of servings : 4

Ingredients:
1.8 litres/3 pints boiling water
1 onion, chopped
225 g/8 oz macaroni
175 g/6 oz Cheddar cheese, grated
300 ml/½ pint milk
2 eggs (size 2), beaten
1 teaspoon made-up mustard
50 g/2 oz Red Leicester cheese, grated
half a packet of crisps, crushed
salt and pepper

Method:
Place in the Casserole Dish the water, onion, macaroni and a little salt. Cover and cook for 12–15 minutes on Full Power or until just tender. Drain off the liquid. Stir in the Cheddar cheese, milk, beaten eggs, mustard and seasoning. Heat for 10 minutes on Full Power, stirring half-way through the cycle. Turn the macaroni into the Shallow Dish. Sprinkle with the Red Leicester cheese and heat for a further 5 minutes on Full Power. Garnish with the crushed crisps before serving.

Serve: with toast.

Variation: add ham, bacon or tomatoes.

Stuffed Jacket Potatoes

Cooking container : Roasting Rack
Cooking time : 21½–22 minutes
Number of servings : 4

Ingredients:
50 g/2 oz bacon
4 medium-size potatoes (each weighing 175–225 g/6–8 oz)
85 g/3½ oz cream cheese
2 tomatoes, skinned
salt and pepper

Method:
Cook the bacon on the Roasting Rack for 1½–2 minutes on Full Power. Leave to cool and then chop finely. Place the potatoes on the Roasting Rack and cook, covered with a sheet of kitchen paper towelling, for approximately 15 minutes on Full Power, or until soft. Turn over half-way through the cycle. Slice the tops off the potatoes and scoop out the centres. Mash the potato with the cream cheese. Chop the tomato flesh and mix with the bacon into the potato. Season to taste. Pile the filling back into the potatoes. Return to the Roasting Rack and heat for 5 minutes on Full Power.

Serve: individually or as part of a meal, e.g., with burgers or spare ribs.

Variation: to cook just one jacket potato (weighing 175 g/6 oz), cook for approximately 5 minutes on Full Power. Try mixing the cream cheese with prawns, ham or chopped hard-poached egg.

Oven Chips

Cooking container : Browning Dish or Shallow Dish
Cooking time : See chart
Number of servings : 1–4

Ingredients:
frozen oven chips

Stuffed Jacket Potatoes

Method:
Heat the Browning Dish for 6 minutes on Full Power. Place the chips in the Dish and heat for the time suggested in the table below. Turn the chips over half-way through the cooking time.

Size of portion	Cooking time
100 g/4 oz	5 minutes
450 g/1 lb	7–8 minutes

Serve: on their own, with a snack meal or with dinner.

Variation: heat 100 g/4 oz chips for 4–5 minutes in the Shallow Dish; 450 g/1 lb chips for 6–7 minutes. Turn over half-way through the cooking time.

Creamed Mushrooms on Toast ★

Cooking container : Shallow Dish
Cooking time   : 8 minutes
Number of servings : 3–4

Ingredients:
450 g/1 lb small button mushrooms
25 g/1 oz butter
1 tablespoon flour
1/2 teaspoon dried herbs
150 ml/1/4 pint creamy milk
salt and pepper

Method:
Wash and dry the mushrooms. Place the butter and the mushrooms in the Shallow Dish and cook, covered, for 4 minutes on Full Power. Stir in the flour, herbs, salt and pepper. Cook for 1 minute on Full Power. Stir in the milk and cook uncovered for 3 minutes on Full Power. Stir well once during cooking and on removal from the cooker.

Serve: on toast or as a vegetable dish.

Note: if this dish is to go in the freezer, the toast should be frozen separately.

French Onion Soup ★

Cooking container   : Casserole Dish
Cooking time   : 40 minutes
Number of servings : 4–5

Ingredients:
450 g/1 lb onions, sliced finely
25 g/1 oz butter
1.2 litres/2 pints beef stock
1 tablespoon flour
salt and pepper

Method:
Place in the Casserole Dish the onions and the butter; then cook, covered, for 15 minutes on Medium Power. Pour in the stock, season, cover and cook on Full Power for 20 minutes. Mix the flour to a smooth paste with a little water. Pour into the soup and cook for a further 5 minutes on Full Power.

Serve: with toasted french bread and with melted cheese on top.

Packet Soup

Cooking container   : Jug
Cooking time   : 11 minutes
Number of servings : 4–5

Ingredients:
900 ml/1½-pint soup packet of your choice
900 ml/1½ pints water

Method:
Empty the contents of the soup packet into the Jug. Gradually stir in the water and ensure the soup is well mixed. Heat in the cooker for 11 minutes on Full Power, stirring every 3 minutes.

Serve: sprinkled with croûtons, toasted in the microwave.

Stuffed Sage and Onion Sausages ★

Cooking containers : Jug/Roasting Rack
Cooking time   : 8½–11½ minutes, plus 20 minutes
                    standing time
Number of servings : 4–8

Ingredients:
150 ml/¼ pint water
50 g/2 oz dry sage and onion stuffing mix
8 pork sausages, cooked
75 g/3 oz Cheddar cheese, grated
8 rashers of thinly cut streaky bacon

Method:
Heat the water in the Jug until boiling (1½–2½ minutes on Full
Power). Stir in the stuffing and leave to stand for 20 minutes.
Slit the sausages almost in half lengthways. Mix the cheese with
the stuffing. Fill the sausages with the mixture and wrap the
bacon around. Heat on the Roasting Rack for 7–9 minutes on
Full Power or until well heated through.

Serve: as a snack or with vegetables and jacket potatoes as a
main meal.

Cheese and Tomato Charlotte ★

Cooking container : Cake Dish
Cooking time   : 12–15 minutes, plus 30 minutes
                     standing time
Number of servings : 4–5

Ingredients:
8 slices of white bread, buttered
225 g/8 oz tomatoes, sliced thinly
100 g/4 oz Red Leicester cheese, grated
100 g/4 oz Cheddar cheese, grated
3 eggs (size 2)
1 teaspoon made-up mustard
600 ml/1 pint milk
salt and pepper

Method:
Place in the Cake Dish a layer of bread; then add the tomatoes and sprinkle with a third of the mixed grated cheeses. Repeat this layering until all the ingredients are used, finishing with cheese. Mix the eggs with seasoning, the mustard and the milk. Pour over the cheese. Leave to stand for 30 minutes before cooking. Cook for 12–15 minutes on Full Power or until firm.

Serve: sprinkled with crushed crisps and with a green side salad.

Cream of Vegetable Soup ★

Cooking container   : Casserole Dish
Cooking time   : 44 minutes
Number of servings : 6

Ingredients:
550 g/1¼ lb frozen mixed vegetables (e.g., spinach, carrots and cauliflower)
50 ml/2 fl oz water
25 g/1 oz butter
2 tablespoons flour
300 ml/½ pint milk
300 ml/½ pint chicken stock
salt and pepper

Method:
Cook the assortment of frozen vegetables with the water in the Casserole Dish, covered, for 18 minutes on Full Power. Cool and purée. Wash the Casserole Dish and melt the butter in it for 1 minute on Full Power. Stir in the flour and cook for 30 seconds on Full Power. Gradually stir in the milk and mix until smooth. Cook for 4½ minutes on Full Power. Stir with a whisk twice during this cycle. Whisk in the stock and seasoning. Add the purée and heat, covered, for 20 minutes on Full Power or to a temperature of 90°C/190°F. Stir before serving.

Serve: with croûtons, toasted in the microwave.

Savoury Stuffed Eggs

Cooking containers : Mini Dishes/Roasting Rack Base
(optional)
Cooking time : 5–8 minutes
Number of servings : 3 as a snack or 6 as a starter

Ingredients:
6 eggs (size 2)
40 g/1½ oz cheese, grated
40 g/1½ oz fresh white breadcrumbs
2 rashers of bacon, cooked and chopped
1 teaspoon mixed herbs
2–3 tablespoons double cream
salt and pepper

Method:
Break the eggs into the Mini Dishes and prick the yolks with a skewer. Place in the Roasting Rack Base or in a circle on the cooker tray. Cook on Medium Power for 2–3 minutes. Scoop out the egg yolks and mix them with the cheese, breadcrumbs, chopped bacon and herbs. Season and bind together with the cream to make a firm stuffing. Refill the eggs with this mixture and heat in the cooker until warm, approximately 3–5 minutes on Full Power.

Serve: 1 per person as a starter or 2 per person as a snack.

Baked Beans on Toast

Cooking container : Vegetable Dish
Cooking time : 5 minutes
Number of servings : 2–3

Ingredients:
450 g/15.9 oz can of baked beans
2–3 slices of bread

Method:
Empty the beans into the Vegetable Dish. Heat for 5 minutes on Full Power. (Temperature Probe setting 85°C/185°F.) Toast the bread while the beans are cooking. Stir the beans, before serving on the toast.

Country Terrine ★

Cooking container   : Loaf Dish
Cooking time   : 20–25 minutes, plus overnight chilling
Number of servings : 8–12

Ingredients:
375 g/13 oz streaky bacon
1 onion, chopped
1 clove of garlic, chopped
375 g/13 oz lean pork, minced
225 g/8 oz pig's liver, minced
100 g/4 oz fresh brown breadcrumbs
2 teaspoons parsley
salt and pepper

Method:
Remove the rind from the bacon. Line the base and sides of the Loaf Dish with 250 g/9 oz of the bacon. Chop the remainder roughly. Mix together well with all the remaining ingredients. Place in the Loaf Dish, taking care not to disturb the bacon. Cook covered with Cling Film for 20–25 minutes on Medium Power or until the terrine is coming away from the sides and the juices are clear when the meat is pressed. Remove the Cling Film, wrap the Dish loosely with foil and weight down the top. Leave overnight in the refrigerator.

Serve: unwrap and turn out; then serve sliced with french bread and salad.

Chicken Drumsticks ★

Cooking container   : Roasting Rack
Cooking time   : 15–17 minutes, plus 5 minutes
                         standing time
Number of servings : 4–8

Ingredients:
8 chicken drumsticks
butter
microwave chicken seasoning

Method:
Place the chicken drumsticks on the Roasting Rack, thin ends towards the centre. Brush with a little melted butter and sprinkle with the microwave chicken seasoning. Cover with a slit Roasting Bag. Cook for 15–17 minutes on Full Power. Stand for 5 minutes before serving.

Serve: with warmed pitta bread and salad or as part of a main meal.

Variation: serve cold with salad.

Beefburgers Stuffed with Stilton ★

Cooking container   : Roasting Rack
Cooking time   : 6–7 minutes
Number of servings : 4

Ingredients:
450 g/1 lb minced beef
1 onion, chopped finely
1 egg (size 3), beaten
1 tablespoon chopped parsley
40 g/1½ oz Stilton cheese
salt and pepper
microwave beef seasoning

Method:
Combine the minced beef, chopped onion, beaten egg and the chopped parsley. Season well. Form into 4 rounds. Chop the Stilton cheese up roughly. Form a well in the centre of each burger, divide the cheese and place in the wells; then form back into burgers. Place on the Roasting Rack and sprinkle with a little microwave seasoning. Cook for 6–7 minutes on Full Power.

Serve: in a bap with a slice of onion and tomato, with salad and jacket potatoes, and dressed with soured cream.

Variation: omit the Stilton and add 50 g/2 oz of roughly chopped peanuts to the original mix.

Beefburgers Stuffed with Stilton; Country Terrine;
Chicken Drumsticks

Reheating snack meals

These timings refer to shop-bought items and are approximate.

Food	Weight/size	Approximate cooking time on Full Power	Instructions
Soup	210 ml/7 fl oz	2½–3½ minutes	stir before serving
Baked beans	100 g/4 oz	1¼–2 minutes	stir before serving
Baked beans	225 g/8 oz	3–4 minutes	stir before serving
Baked beans	450 g/1 lb	5–6 minutes	stir before serving
Ravioli	200 g/7 oz	3½–4½ minutes	stir before serving
Ravioli	450 g/1 lb	6–7 minutes	stir before serving
Pizza	10 cm/4 inches	2 minutes	heat on Roasting Rack
Chicken portion	225 g/8 oz	2½ minutes	heat on Roasting Rack
4 Chicken portions	900 g/2 lb	8–10 minutes	heat on Roasting Rack
Sausages	450 g/1 lb	4½–5½ minutes	heat on Roasting Rack

1 Beefburger in bun		45 seconds	heat on Roasting Rack
4 Beefburgers in buns		2–3 minutes	heat on Roasting Rack
1 Hot dog in roll		30–45 seconds	heat on Roasting Rack
4 Hot dogs in rolls		2–2½ minutes	heat on Roasting Rack
Meat pie	single size	1–1½ minutes	heat on Roasting Rack
Meat pie	family size	4½–6 minutes	heat on Roasting Rack
Quiche	single size	1–1½ minutes	heat on Roasting Rack
Quiche	family size	5–6 minutes	heat on Roasting Rack
3 Fish fingers		1–1½ minutes	heat on Roasting Rack
10 Fish fingers		2½–3 minutes	heat on Roasting Rack
Lasagne	single size	3½–4½ minutes	heat on suitable dish
Lasagne	family size	15–18 minutes	heat on suitable dish

Dinner

These dinner recipes are all substantial dishes, many of which take less than 30 minutes to cook. Other recipes do take longer, but can be prepared in advance and reheated quickly as required. There is a vegetable cooking chart, which covers many varieties. Try cooking rice and pasta in the microwave cooker to accompany some of the main dishes, as they make a nice change from potatoes. Since all the family like puddings, I have included some of my favourites!

Tropical Chicken ★

Cooking container : Shallow Dish
Cooking time : 31–36 minutes
Number of servings : 4

Ingredients:
4 chicken quarters
1 medium-size green pepper, sliced
1 medium-size onion, chopped
15 g/½ oz butter
100 g/4 oz tenderised apricots
150 ml/¼ pint stock
439 g/15½ oz can of pineapple rings
salt and pepper

Method:
Pre-brown the chicken under a grill or in a frying pan. Place into the Shallow Dish the pepper, onion and butter. Cook covered for 6 minutes on Medium Power. Add the chicken and apricots to the Dish. Pour over the stock and the juice from the can of pineapple. Cook covered for 20–25 minutes on Full Power or until the chicken is cooked. Add the pineapple rings, season and heat for a further 5 minutes on Full Power.

Serve: with rice, noodles or potato bake and with a green vegetable.

Country Bacon Joint; Tropical Chicken with noodles; Lamb Curry with rice

Country Bacon Joint ★

Cooking container : Casserole Dish
Cooking time   : 30–38 minutes, plus 20 minutes
                     standing time
Number of servings : 6–8

Ingredients:
1.25–1.3 kg/2½–3 lb piece of bacon (suitable for boiling)
1.8 litres/3 pints water
1 onion, sliced
2 carrots, sliced
1 bay leaf
a few peppercorns

Method:
Place the bacon, water, vegetables, bay leaf and peppercorns in the Casserole Dish and cook on Full Power for 30–38 minutes or until the internal temperature of the bacon reaches 65°C/150°F. Remove the bacon from the stock and wrap in foil for 20 minutes. Remove the skin before serving.

Serve: with potatoes and carrots, or with onions and a mustard sauce.

Lamb Curry ★

Cooking container : Casserole Dish
Cooking time   : 56 minutes
Number of servings : 4–5

Ingredients:
550 g/1¼ lb raw leg or shoulder of lamb
2 medium-size onions, sliced
1 tablespoon oil
4 heaped teaspoons curry powder (medium hot)
2 tablespoons lemon juice
2 tablespoons mango chutney
2 tablespoons tomato purée
298 g/10.6 oz can of condensed lentil soup
hot water
1 large cooking apple, sliced

Method:
Cut the meat into 2.5 cm/1-inch cubes. Seal and colour in a frying pan. Cook the onion with the oil, covered, in the Casserole Dish for 5 minutes on Medium Power. Stir in the curry powder and cook covered for a further minute on Full Power. Stir in the lemon juice, chutney, tomato purée, soup and 1½ soup cans of hot water. Add the apple and lamb and cook covered for 10 minutes on Full Power; then cook for 40 minutes on Medium Power or until the lamb is tender. Leave to stand before serving.

Serve: with rice, sliced bananas, peanuts and poppadams. To heat 3 poppadams, place on the oven tray, cook on Full Power for 45 seconds, rearrange and cook for a further 45 seconds.

Variation: add sultanas or coconut to the curry.

Pork Chops with Apple ★

Cooking container	: Shallow Dish
Cooking time	: 13–15 minutes, plus 5 minutes standing time
Number of servings	: 4

Ingredients:
4 good-size pork chops
1 large cooking apple
25 g/1 oz butter
lemon juice
2 tablespoons demerara sugar
microwave seasoning

Method:
Pre-brown the chops under a grill. Place in the Shallow Dish. Peel and core the apple and slice into 4 rings. Top the pork chops with the apple rings, smear over the butter, squeeze with lemon juice and sprinkle with the sugar and microwave seasoning. Cook covered for 3 minutes on Full Power and then for 10–12 minutes on Medium Power or until the pork is tender. Stand for 5 minutes before serving.

Serve: with celery in a basil sauce and with potatoes.

Steak and Kidney Pudding

Cooking containers : Vegetable Dish/Disposable Pudding
Basin
Cooking time : 1 hour 55–57 minutes
Number of servings : 4

Ingredients:
450 g/1 lb stewing steak
225 g/8 oz pig's kidney
1 tablespoon oil
1 onion, chopped
2 tablespoons plain flour
water
225 g/8 oz suet pastry
chopped parsley
salt and pepper

Method:
Cut the beef and kidney into neat cubes. Place the oil, meat and
chopped onion in the Vegetable Dish, cover and cook for 8
minutes on Full Power. Stir in the flour, season and add 4
tablespoons of water. Cover and cook on Low Power for 1 hour
40 minutes. Stir occasionally.

Line the greased Basin with 2 cm/¾ inch of the pastry. Fill
the Basin with the meat. Add 4 tablespoons water. Top with the
remaining pastry and seal the edges. Cover loosely with Cling
Film and cook on Full Power for 7–9 minutes. Turn out, and
sprinkle with the parsley.

Serve: with boiled potatoes, peas and carrots.

Variation: use mushrooms instead of kidneys and substitute
red wine for the water.

Sweet and Sour Chicken ★

Cooking container : Shallow Dish
Cooking time : 17 minutes
Number of servings : 3–4

Ingredients:
1 large onion
1 green pepper
2 carrots
1 tablespoon oil
2 tablespoons dry sherry
1 tablespoon tomato purée
2 tablespoons soy sauce
1 tablespoon red wine vinegar
5 tablespoons sugar
1 tablespoon cornflour
175 ml/6 fl oz water
350 g/12 oz chicken, cooked
salt and pepper

Method:
Cut the onion, pepper and carrots into 4 cm/1½-inch long thin strips and place in the Shallow Dish. Add the oil, cover and cook for 5 minutes on Full Power. Stir in the sherry, tomato purée, soy sauce, vinegar and sugar. Mix the cornflour to a smooth paste with a little of the water. Add to the Shallow Dish with the remaining water. Cook uncovered for 5 minutes on Full Power, stirring after 2½ minutes. Stir in the chicken, season and heat for 7 minutes on Full Power. Stir before serving.

Serve: with noodles or with rice and a few crispy noodles.

Variation: use cooked pork or prawns instead of chicken.

Cod Mornay ★

Cooking containers : Shallow Dish/Jug
Cooking time : 18–21 minutes, plus 5 minutes
standing time
Number of servings : 4–5

Ingredients:
675 g/1½ lb cod fillets, skinned
25 g/1 oz butter
25 g/1 oz plain flour
½ teaspoon dry mustard
300 ml/½ pint milk
75 g/3 oz cheese, grated
2 tomatoes, sliced
salt and pepper

Method:
Place the cod fillets in the Shallow Dish, overlapping the tail ends and thinner edges of the fish. Melt the butter in the Jug for 1 minute on Full Power. Stir in the flour and mustard; then cook for 1 minute on Full Power. Gradually whisk in the milk. Cook for 3 minutes on Full Power. Whisk in the cheese and seasoning. Pour over the fish. Garnish with the sliced tomatoes. Heat covered for 13–16 minutes or until the fish flakes. Stand for 5 minutes before serving.

Serve: with mashed or duchesse potatoes and a green salad.

Variation: use any fish of your choice and serve sprinkled with crushed crisps.

Beef and Tomato Casserole ★

Cooking container : Casserole Dish
Cooking time   : approximately 3 hours
Number of servings : 5–6

Ingredients:
225 g/8 oz carrots, chopped
2 sticks of celery, chopped
1 large onion, chopped
2 tablespoons oil
900 g/2 lb stewing beef, cut into cubes
2 tablespoons plain flour
1 teaspoon dry mustard
397 g/14 oz can of tomatoes, chopped
2 tablespoons tomato purée
300 ml/½ pint beef stock
salt and pepper

Method:

Place the chopped carrot, celery, onion and oil in the Casserole Dish. Cook covered for 7 minutes on Medium Power. Stir in the meat and cook covered on Full Power for 10 minutes. Stir once during the cycle. Mix in the flour and mustard, chopped tomatoes, tomato purée, stock, salt and pepper. Cook covered on Full Power for 15 minutes and then on Low Power for 2½ hours. (Temperature Probe: 90°C/190°F for 3–4 hours.)

Serve: with jacket potatoes or french bread and a green vegetable.

Prawn-stuffed Plaice ★

Cooking containers : Jug/Shallow Dish
Cooking time   : 11¾ minutes–14½ minutes,
                      plus 5 minutes standing time
Number of servings : 4

Ingredients:

75 g/3 oz butter
100 g/4 oz peeled prawns, chopped
50 g/2 oz fresh white breadcrumbs
2 tablespoons single cream
1 tablespoon chopped parsley
8 medium-size plaice fillets, skinned
2 tablespoons lemon juice
1 teaspoon dill weed
1 teaspoon unseasoned microwave colouring
salt and pepper

Method:

Heat 50 g/2 oz butter in the Jug for 1–1½ minutes on Full Power to melt. Stir in the prawns, breadcrumbs, cream and parsley; then season. Divide the stuffing between the fillets of plaice. Roll up each plaice, from the tail end, around the stuffing. Place in the Shallow Dish. Melt the remaining butter for 45 seconds–1 minute on Full Power and then add seasoning, the lemon juice, dill weed and microwave colouring. Pour over the fish. Cook covered for 10–12 minutes on Full Power. Stand for 5 minutes before serving.

Serve: hot with sauté potatoes, carrots and broad beans.

Meat Balls
in Herb and Mushroom Sauce ★

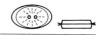

Cooking containers : Roasting Rack/Shallow Dish
Cooking time : 13 minutes
Number of servings : 4

Ingredients:
450 g/1 lb minced beef
100 g/4 oz sausage meat
50 g/2 oz fresh breadcrumbs
½ teaspoon salt
2 tablespoons tomato purée
¼ teaspoon dried marjoram
½ teaspoon dried parsley
1 egg (size 3), beaten
unseasoned microwave colouring

For the sauce:
298 g/10.6 oz can of condensed cream of mushroom soup
water
1 teaspoon ground paprika
½ teaspoon dried parsley

Method:
Combine together the minced beef, sausage meat, bread-crumbs, salt, tomato purée, marjoram, parsley and egg. Form into 12 balls. Place on the Roasting Rack and sprinkle with the colouring. Cover with a slit Roasting Bag. Cook for 8 minutes on Full Power.

Mix the soup with half a soup can of water and add the paprika and parsley. Put in the Shallow Dish and heat for 5 minutes on Full Power. Place in the meat balls, spoon over the sauce and heat on Full Power for 3 minutes.

Serve: with noodles or spaghetti.

Variation: use an alternative flavour of soup as a sauce.

Fresh vegetable cooking chart

All vegetables are cooked on Full Power in the covered Vegetable Dish or Casserole Dish. Do not add salt until after the vegetables are cooked.

Frozen vegetables can also be cooked in the microwave cooker and take approximately the same amount of time as fresh. Many frozen food manufacturers now print cooking instructions on the pack for easy reference. (Home-frozen vegetables will generally take longer.)

Note: All timings are approximate, depending on the freshness, size and preparation of vegetables. All amounts are 450 g/ 1 lb unless stated otherwise.

Vegetable	Preparation	Water (or butter) added	Cooking time	Standing time
Artichokes (225 g/8 oz)	Wash and then shake off excess water; wrap in Cling Film	–	6–10 minutes	4 minutes
Asparagus	Trim	2 tablespoons	8–12 minutes	5 minutes
Aubergines	Peel and dice	4 tablespoons	8–10 minutes	5 minutes
Bean sprouts (350 g/12 oz)	Wash and drain	25 g/1 oz butter	3–5 minutes	2 minutes
Beetroot	Cut in half	4 tablespoons	9–12 minutes	10 minutes
Broad beans	Shell	4 tablespoons	10–15 minutes	5 minutes
Broccoli (225 g/8 oz)	Slice lengthways	4 tablespoons	8–10 minutes	5 minutes
Brussels sprouts (225 g/8 oz)	Trim	4 tablespoons	8–10 minutes	5 minutes
Cabbage	Trim and shred	3 tablespoons	8–10 minutes	5 minutes

Vegetable	Preparation		Steaming time	Microwave time
Carrots	Slice thinly	4 tablespoons	10–12 minutes	5 minutes
Cauliflower (florets)	Separate	4 tablespoons	10–12 minutes	10 minutes
Cauliflower (whole)	Trim outer leaves	6 tablespoons	11–15 minutes	5 minutes
Celery	Cut in 6.5 cm/ 2½-inch pieces	3 tablespoons	10–12 minutes	5 minutes
Courgettes	Slice	A knob of butter	11–12 minutes	5 minutes
Fennel	Slice thinly	1 tablespoon	11–12 minutes	10 minutes
Leeks	Slice into 2.5 cm/ 1-inch pieces	4 tablespoons	8–10 minutes	5 minutes
Button mushrooms (225 g/8 oz)	Wash	25 g/1 oz butter	4–6 minutes	2 minutes
Marrow	Cut in cubes	A knob of butter	8–10 minutes	5 minutes
New potatoes	Cut small	6 tablespoons	10–12 minutes	5 minutes
Onions	Leave whole	2 tablespoons	8–10 minutes	10 minutes
Parsnips	Slice thinly into 5 cm/2-inch pieces	4 tablespoons	10–12 minutes	10 minutes
Peas	Shell	A knob of butter	10–12 minutes	5 minutes
Runner beans	String and slice	4 tablespoons	10–15 minutes	5 minutes
Spinach	Wash	–	7–8 minutes	5 minutes
Spring cabbage	Wash and shred	2 tablespoons	9–12 minutes	10 minutes
Swede	Dice	4 tablespoons	16–18 minutes	10 minutes
Tomatoes	Cut in half	Brush with melted butter	3–5 minutes	10 minutes

Rice ★

Cooking container : Casserole Dish
Cooking time   : 12 minutes
Number of servings : 4

Ingredients:
1.2 litres/2 pints boiling water
175 g/6 oz long grain rice
salt

Method:
Pour the boiling water into the Casserole Dish. Add a little salt and the rice. Cover the Dish and cook in the microwave for 12 minutes on Full Power or until the rice is just soft. Drain and serve.

Variation: to make fried rice, melt 40 g/1½ oz butter in the Shallow Dish. Stir in 350 g/12 oz cooked rice and cook for 5 minutes on Full Power.

Pasta (Noodles) ★

Cooking container : Casserole Dish
Cooking time   : 8 minutes
Number of servings : 4

Ingredients:
1.8 litres/3 pints boiling water
1 tablespoon oil
225 g/8 oz egg noodles
salt

Method:
Pour the boiling water into the Casserole Dish. Add the oil and a little salt. Stir in the noodles. Cover and cook for 8 minutes on Full Power or until the noodles are just soft.

Serve: with a good sprinkling of cheese and a touch of cream, or use instead of potatoes with meat and fish dishes.

Variation: cook all pasta by this method and approximately to the time stated on the pasta packaging.

Fruit Crumble ★

Cooking container	: Roasting Rack Base
Cooking time	: 18–20 minutes, plus 5 minutes standing time
Number of servings	: 4–5

Ingredients:
675 g/1½ lb raw fruit
approximately 100 g/4 oz sugar
grated rind of 1 lemon
30 ml/1 fl oz water
75 g/3 oz butter
150 g/5 oz plain flour
40 g/1½ oz caster sugar
40 g/1½ oz soft brown sugar
50 g/2 oz walnuts

Method:
Prepare the fruit. Place the fruit, sugar, lemon rind and water in the Base. Cover and cook for 5 minutes on Full Power or until the fruit is just softening. Stir on removal from the cooker. Rub the butter into the flour until it resembles fine breadcrumbs. Mix in the sugars. Chop the walnuts finely and mix with the flour. Sprinkle evenly over the fruit. Cook for 13–15 minutes on Full Power. Stand for 5 minutes before serving.

Serve: with custard, cream or ice cream.

Rice Pudding ★

Cooking container	: Vegetable Dish
Cooking time	: 46–53 minutes, plus 10 minutes standing time
Number of servings	: 3–4

Ingredients:
40 g/1½ oz pudding rice
25 g/1 oz caster sugar
600 ml/1 pint milk
ground nutmeg

Method:
Place the rice, sugar and milk in the Vegetable Dish. Cook covered for 6–8 minutes on Full Power or until the milk is just simmering; then cook on Low Power for 40–45 minutes or until the rice is soft. Stand covered for 10 minutes before sprinkling with nutmeg.

Variation: stir in 25 g/1 oz of sultanas 10 minutes before the end of the cooking time.

Grapefruit Upside-down Pudding ★

Cooking container : Cake Dish
Cooking time : 7½–9½ minutes, plus 5 minutes standing time
Number of servings : 6–8

Ingredients:
50 g/2 oz butter
50 g/2 oz soft light brown sugar
425 g/15 oz grapefruit segments
6–8 glacé cherries
150 g/5 oz margarine
150 g/5 oz caster sugar
2 eggs (size 2)
175 g/6 oz self-raising flour
3 tablespoons fruit juice

Method:
Heat the butter in the Cake Dish for 1½ minutes on Full Power. Stir in the soft light brown sugar and spread evenly over the Dish base. Drain and arrange the grapefruit segments and cherries on the sugar in the Dish. Cream the margarine and caster sugar together until soft. Beat in the eggs; then fold in the flour and fruit juice. Spread the mixture evenly over the grapefruit. Cook uncovered for 6–8 minutes on Full Power or until set. Stand for 5 minutes before turning out.

Serve: hot or cold with custard, lemon sauce or cream.

Variation: use any fruit of your choice and flavour the sponge chocolate.

Baked Apples

Cooking container : Flan Dish
Cooking time : 8–10 minutes, plus 5 minutes
standing time
Number of servings : 4

Ingredients:
4 medium-size cooking apples
50 g/2 oz stoned dates, chopped
25 g/1 oz walnuts, chopped
3 tablespoons golden syrup

Method:
Core the apples and score the tops lightly with a sharp knife.
Place in the Flan Dish. Stuff the apples with the dates and
walnuts and spoon over the golden syrup. Cook on Full Power
for 8–10 minutes. Stand for 5 minutes before serving.

Serve: with custard, cream or milk pudding.

Custard

Cooking container : Jug
Cooking time : 6–7½ minutes
Number of servings : 4

Ingredients:
1–2 tablespoons custard powder
600 ml/1 pint milk
2 tablespoons sugar

Method:
Mix the custard powder to a smooth paste with a little of the
milk in the Jug. Stir in the sugar and the remaining milk. Cook
for 6–7½ minutes on Full Power or until the custard begins to
boil. Stir well every 2 minutes.

Serve: with puddings and fruit.

Variation: for Banana Custard, add 2 sliced bananas before
serving. For Chocolate Custard, add 25 g/1 oz cocoa powder to
the mixture.

Mini Jam Sponge Puddings ★

Cooking containers : 6 Mini Dishes
Cooking time   : 5½–8½ minutes
Number of servings : 9

Ingredients:
100 g/4 oz margarine
100 g/4 oz caster sugar
2 eggs (size 3)
100 g/4 oz plain flour
1 teaspoon baking powder
1 tablespoon hot water
9 heaped tablespoons jam

Method:
Cream the margarine and sugar together until light. Beat in the
eggs and fold in the combined flour and baking powder. Add
the hot water. Lightly grease the Mini Dishes. Put a heaped
spoon of jam in the base of each and fill each three-quarters full
with the mixture. Cover loosely with Cling Film and cook for
3½–5½ minutes on Full Power or until the sponges are set.
Turn out and refill 3 of the Dishes in the same way. Cook these
for 2–3 minutes on Full Power.

Serve: with jam sauce or custard.

Custard; Baked Apples; Mini Jam Sponge Puddings

Tea time

Tea time, coffee time, any time: cakes, bread and buns are always welcome and their cooking time in the microwave cooker is so short you really can cope with unexpected visitors. Also included is a heating chart for tea time treats and, to go with the bread, scones or crumpets, a delicious Orange Curd recipe.

Wholewheat Bread

Cooking containers : Jug/Loaf Dish
Cooking time : 23–29 minutes, including standing and kneading
Number of servings : 10–12

Ingredients:
300 ml/½ pint water
1 teaspoon caster sugar
2 teaspoons dried yeast
450 g/1 lb wholewheat bread flour
½ teaspoon salt
15 g/½ oz butter
a little oil
bran, poppy or sesame seeds

Method:
Heat the water in the Jug for 1 minute on Full Power. Mix the sugar with the yeast and the water. Stand for 10 minutes until frothy. Combine together the flour and salt. Rub in the butter. Gradually work in the yeast and water, mixing to a dough. Knead on a floured surface for 5–10 minutes until smooth and elastic. Place in a greased bowl, cover and leave to rise until double the size. Re-knead the dough, shape and place in the lightly greased Loaf Dish. Leave in a plastic bag until the dough has risen. Remove from the bag and brush lightly with oil. Sprinkle with bran, poppy or sesame seeds. Cook on Full Power for 7–8 minutes. Turn out and allow to cool on a wire rack.

Variation: add 1 tablespoon of mixed herbs and 1 tablespoon of chopped onions to make Herb Bread.

Tea time heating chart

Food item and quantity	Heating time on Full Power
4 Butter crumpets	1½–2 minutes
6 Scones	1 minute or 2 minutes from frozen
6 Mince pies	1 minute or 2 minutes from frozen
6 Doughnuts	45 seconds
4 Danish pastries	45 seconds–1½ minutes

Defrosting bread	
Quantity	Heating time on Low (Defrost) Power
1 large sliced loaf	8–10 minutes cooking (separate into 2 piles as soon as possible); 10–15 minutes standing

Victoria Sandwich ★

Cooking container : Cake Dish
Cooking time : 5–6 minutes, plus 5 minutes standing time
Number of servings : 6–8

Ingredients:
175 g/6 oz margarine or butter
175 g/6 oz caster sugar
175 g/6 oz plain flour
2½ teaspoons baking powder
2 tablespoons warm water
3 eggs (size 2), beaten

Method:
Combine all the ingredients in a mixing bowl. Mix until smooth. Line the base of the Dish with Layering Tissue or greased greaseproof paper. Lightly grease the sides of the Dish. Pour the mix into the Dish and even out the top. Cook in the microwave for 5–6 minutes on Full Power. Stand for 5 minutes before turning out to cool.

Serve: split the cake in half (horizontally) when cold and fill with jam and cream. Dust the top with icing or caster sugar.

American Nut Brownies ★

Cooking containers : Jug/Roasting Rack Base
Cooking time : 7–8 minutes
Number of servings : 8–10

Ingredients:
2 eggs (size 2)
225 g/8 oz granulated sugar
½ teaspoon salt
1 teaspoon vanilla essence
100 g/4 oz butter
75 g/3 oz self-raising flour, sifted
50 g/2 oz cocoa
100 g/4 oz chopped nuts

Method:
Beat together the eggs, sugar, salt and vanilla essence until light and creamy. Melt the butter in the Jug for 1 minute on Full Power and stir into the mixture. Fold in the sifted flour and cocoa and then the chopped nuts. Line the Base of the Roasting Rack with Layering Tissue or greased greaseproof paper. Pour the mixture into the Base and even out. Cook for 6–7 minutes on Full Power or until firm to the touch. Cool in the Base and cut into sections.

Variation: top with chocolate butter icing or melted chocolate.

Meringues ★

Cooking containers : Mini Dishes
Cooking time : 3–4 minutes
Number of servings : 15

Ingredients:
1 egg white (size 2)
275 g/10 oz icing sugar, sifted

Method:
Whisk the egg white until firm. Stir in the icing sugar to form a stiff mix and divide into 15 balls. Place each ball in a paper case.

American Nut Brownies; Wholewheat Bread; Victoria Sandwich

Put the paper cases into the Mini Dishes. Cook 6 at a time on Full Power for 1½ minutes or until the meringue sets. Repeat until all are cooked.

Variation: flavour and colour the meringues with liquids, e.g. strawberry flavour and cochineal, chocolate flavouring and colouring or peppermint flavouring and green colouring.

Shortbread

Cooking container   : Flan Dish
Cooking time   : 3–4 minutes
Number of servings : 8

Ingredients:
100 g/4 oz butter
50 g/2 oz caster sugar, plus extra for sprinkling
100 g/4 oz plain flour
50 g/2 oz rice flour
grated rind of 1 orange

Method:
Cream the butter with the sugar until fluffy. Work in the flour, rice flour and orange rind. Press the mix into the Flan Dish. Prick and mark with a fork. Cook for 3–4 minutes on Full Power. Remove from the cooker, mark into wedges and sprinkle with extra caster sugar. Leave in the dish to cool.

Walnut Flapjacks

Cooking containers : Jug/Flan Dish
Cooking time   : 4¾ minutes
Number of servings : 8

Ingredients:
80 ml/3 fl oz golden syrup
75 g/3 oz butter
100 g/4 oz soft brown sugar
175 g/6 oz jumbo or porridge oats
50 g/2 oz chopped walnuts
a good pinch of salt

Method:
Into the Jug place the golden syrup, butter and sugar. Heat in the microwave cooker for 1½ minutes on Full Power. Stir in the oats, walnuts and salt. Turn the mix into the lightly greased and lined Flan Dish and even out. Cook for 3 minutes 15 seconds on Full Power. Mark into 8 pieces while hot. Turn out and cut into sections when cool.

Variation: omit the walnuts and stir in 50 g/2 oz sultanas instead.

Sultana Fairy Cakes ★

Cooking containers : Mini Dishes/Roasting Rack
                        Base (optional)
Cooking time   : 4½–6 minutes
Number of servings : 18–20

Ingredients:
100 g/4 oz butter
100 g/4 oz caster sugar
2 eggs (size 2)
100 g/4 oz self-raising flour
50 g/2 oz sultanas
2 tablespoons warm water

Method:
Cream the butter and the sugar until fluffy. Gradually beat in the eggs. Fold in the flour and sultanas and then the water. Place paper cases into the Mini Dishes. Half fill the cases with the mix. Cook 6 at a time, either placed to form a circle on the base of the cooker or using the Base of the Roasting Rack as a tray. Cook for 1½–2 minutes on Full Power or until the cakes are firm. Remove the cakes from the Mini Dishes and repeat until all the mix is used.

Serve: decorated with icing and crystallised violets.

Variation: add a little grated lemon or orange rind or chopped glacé cherries instead of sultanas. Try decorating with glacé icing and halved glacé cherries.

Chocolate Gâteau

Cooking containers : 3 Disposable Pie Plates
Cooking time : 5–6 minutes
Number of servings : 6–8

Ingredients:
100 g/4 oz margarine
100 g/4 oz caster sugar
2 eggs (size 2)
4 tablespoons golden syrup
100 g/4 oz plain flour, sifted
50 g/2 oz ground almonds
50 g/2 oz cocoa
2 teaspoons baking powder
4 tablespoons milk
300 ml/½ pint double cream
375 g/12 oz plain chocolate
312 g/11 oz can of mandarins

Method:
Cream the margarine and sugar together until light and fluffy. Beat in the eggs and stir in the golden syrup. Fold in the sifted flour, ground almonds, cocoa and baking powder. Stir in the milk.

Line the Pie Plates with Layering Tissue or greased greaseproof paper. Divide the mix between the Plates and spread out. Cook each layer, one at a time, for approximately 2½–3 minutes on Full Power. Turn out on to a wire rack to cool. Heat the cream until just boiling (2½–3 minutes on Full Power). Stir in the chocolate and mix gently until all the chocolate is melted. Leave the cream to cool. Spoon a little of the fruit juice from the can over each layer of sponge. Whisk half the chocolate cream until thickened; then spread quickly over the bottom layer of sponge. Top with the second layer and spread with the double cream and the drained mandarins. Cover with the third layer of sponge and a thin layer of cream. Pour the remaining half of the chocolate cream over the top and sides of the cake. Spread with a palette knife. (If the chocolate has set, reheat for a few seconds.)

Sultana Fairy Cakes; Chocolate Gâteau; Walnut Flapjacks

Orange Curd

Cooking container : Casserole Dish
Cooking time   : 13–17 minutes
Number of servings : Makes 900 g/2 lb

Ingredients:
2 large oranges
100 g/4 oz butter
450 g/1 lb caster sugar
4 eggs (size 2)

Method:
Grate the oranges and extract the juice; then place both the peel and juice in the Casserole Dish. Add the butter and sugar. Heat uncovered for 7–9 minutes on Full Power or until the sugar is dissolved. Stir once during this cycle and on removal from the cooker. Beat the eggs into the orange mix. Cook for 6–8 minutes on Medium Power or until the curd thickens. Stir once during this cycle. Pour into two 450 g/1 lb sterilised jars. Pot as normal and leave to cool. Store in a refrigerator.

Variation: for Lemon Curd, use the juice and grated rind of 3 lemons.

Sunday lunch

Sunday lunch is for many households the one occasion when the whole family sits around the table to enjoy a meal together. For this traditional meal you can combine the speed of the microwave cooker with the conventional oven to give the food its expected appearance.

Try cooking the Sunday joint or poultry in the microwave cooker and then place in the oven (for the usual standing time) to give a crisp finish. Use the microwave cooker for vegetable dishes (see pages 54–55 for cooking times), sauces and gravies. Parboil potatoes in the microwave cooker and then cook in the conventional oven (cook a few extra to reheat on Monday). Yorkshire pudding is, however, best not microwaved. Sunday puddings are easily cooked in the microwave.

Cooking joints of meat

Joints of meat cooked in the microwave are moist and full of flavour. Place the joint of meat on the Roasting Rack: this helps the meat to cook evenly, since it is not cooking in its own juices. Sprinkle with seasoned or unseasoned microwave colouring or your own recipe. (Try a combination of some of the following: sherry, soy sauce, Marmite, honey, paprika and Worcestershire sauce.) Cover with a slit Roasting Bag and cook in the microwave for the suggested time. Large joints should be turned over once during cooking.

For accurate meat cooking it is well worth investing in a microwave thermometer. This is inserted into the centre of the meat. When the correct internal temperature is reached, remove from the cooker and leave to stand. Wrap the meat in foil or place in a warm oven for additional colouring and crispness. When placing the thermometer into the meat, avoid touching the bone. Do NOT place a conventional thermometer into the microwave cooker.

Poultry is cooked by the same method. If using a thermometer, push into the thickest part of the thigh. When the correct temperature is reached, insert the thermometer into the other side of the bird and check that the temperature is the same.

Meat cooking chart: approximate time per 450 g/1 lb

Meat	Cooking time on Full Power	Internal temperature on removal from oven	Instructions
Beef	Rare : 5–6 minutes Medium : 7–8 minutes Well done : 8–10 minutes	55°C/130°F 65°C/150°F 70°C/160°F	Stand covered in foil for 15–20 minutes before serving.
Lamb/Veal	7–9 minutes	75°C/170°F	Stand covered in foil for 15–25 minutes before serving.
Pork	7–9 minutes	80°C/175°F	Stand covered in foil for 15–25 minutes before serving.
Gammon	7–8 minutes	65°C/150°F	Stand covered in foil for 15–20 minutes before serving.

Poultry cooking chart: approximate time per 450 g/1 lb

Poultry	Cooking time on Full Power	Instructions
Chicken (whole)	6–8 minutes	Stand wrapped in foil for 15–20 minutes before serving.
Chicken (portions)	6–7 minutes	Arrange on the Roasting Rack, thick ends towards the outer edge. Stand for 5–10 minutes before serving.
Duck (whole)	7–9 minutes	Stand wrapped in foil for 15–20 minutes before serving.
Capon	6–8 minutes	Start cooking breast-side down and turn over half-way through the cooking time. Stand wrapped in foil for 15–20 minutes before serving.
Turkey	6–8 minutes	Start cooking breast-side down and turn over half-way through the cooking time. Stand wrapped in foil for 15–20 minutes before serving.

Bread Sauce ★

Cooking container : Jug
Cooking time : 10–11 minutes, plus 15 minutes
standing time
Number of servings : 4–5

Ingredients:
300 ml/½ pint milk
1 small onion, peeled
2 cloves
1 bay leaf
40 g/1½ oz fresh white breadcrumbs
15 g/½ oz butter
salt and pepper

Method:
Place the milk, the onion stuck with the cloves and the bay leaf in the Jug. Heat for 3–4 minutes on Full Power; then leave to stand for 15 minutes. Stir in the breadcrumbs and butter and cook for 7 minutes on Medium Power. Remove the bay leaf and onion. Season to taste.

Serve: with turkey, chicken or ham.

Gravy ★

Cooking container : Jug
Cooking time : 4–5 minutes
Number of servings : 4

Ingredients:
1 tablespoon plain flour
3 tablespoons juices from the meat
300 ml/½ pint stock
gravy browning

Method:
Mix the flour with the meat juices until smooth and heat for 1 minute on Full Power. Whisk in the stock and cook in the cooker on Full Power for 3–4 minutes or until the gravy boils. Add gravy browning as required to colour.

White Sauce ★

Cooking container : Jug
Cooking time   : 5–6 minutes
Number of servings : 4

Ingredients:
25 g/1 oz butter
25 g/1 oz plain flour
300 ml/½ pint milk
salt and pepper

Method:
Melt the butter in the Jug for 1 minute on Full Power. Stir in the flour and cook for 1 minute on Full Power. Gradually whisk in the milk. Return the Jug to the cooker. Heat on Full Power for 3–4 minutes or until the sauce begins to boil, whisking after 2 minutes and on removal from the cooker. Season to taste.

Stuffing for Poultry ★

Cooking container : Jug
Cooking time   : 5 minutes
Number of servings : 4

Ingredients:
1 stick of celery, chopped
1 onion, chopped
2 eating apples, cored and chopped
15 g/½ oz butter
40 g/1½ oz fresh breadcrumbs
grated rind of 1 lemon
salt and pepper

Method:
Into the Jug place the celery, onion and apples. Add the butter and cook for 5 minutes on Medium Power. Stir in the breadcrumbs, lemon rind and salt and pepper. Stuff your bird in the required method.

Variation: add seasoning and other ingredients, such as sultanas and peanuts, as required.

West Country Red Cabbage ★

Cooking container : Casserole Dish
Cooking time : 50 minutes
Number of servings : 4–6

Ingredients:
675 g/1½ lb red cabbage
1 large cooking apple
1 large onion
50 g/2 oz butter
2 tablespoons golden syrup
110 ml/4 fl oz cider vinegar

Method:
Shred the cabbage finely, peel and chop the apple and skin the onion. Place in the Casserole Dish the cabbage, butter and golden syrup; then cover and cook for 10 minutes on Medium Power. Stir in the vinegar, apple and onion. Cover and cook for 40 minutes on Medium Power.

Serve: with ham or pork dishes.

Green Beans Almondine

Cooking containers : Vegetable Dish/Shallow Dish
Cooking time : 18–20 minutes
Number of servings : 4–5

Ingredients:
450 g/1 lb whole, green beans
6 tablespoons water
1 clove of garlic, crushed
50 g/2 oz butter
50 g/2 oz flaked almonds
salt and pepper

Method:
Place the beans and water in the Vegetable Dish and cook on Full Power for 12 minutes or until the beans are tender. Drain

West Country Red Cabbage; Green Beans Almondine; Celery with Basil Sauce

and leave to stand, covered. Place the garlic, butter and almonds in the Shallow Dish and cook uncovered until the almonds are browned, about 6–8 minutes. Stir frequently. Mix the beans into the almonds and sprinkle with seasoning.

Variation: serve the almond and butter mixture on top of cauliflower or broccoli.

Celery with Basil Sauce ★

Cooking containers : Vegetable Dish/Jug
Cooking time : 20¾ minutes
Number of servings : 4–5

Ingredients:
1 head of celery
110 ml/4 fl oz water
approximately 210 ml/7 fl oz milk
1 small onion, chopped finely
25 g/1 oz butter
1 tablespoon plain flour
1 teaspoon chopped basil
salt and pepper

Method:
Clean the celery, removing any string or dry bits. Cut into 7.5 cm/3-inch pieces. Place in the Vegetable Dish with the water. Cook covered for 10 minutes 15 seconds on Full Power or until tender. (Rearrange the celery after 6 minutes.) Drain off the liquid and top up to 300 ml/½ pint with milk. Place the onion and butter in the Jug and cook for 5 minutes on Medium Power. Stir in the flour and cook for 30 seconds on Full Power. Gradually mix in the milk, basil, salt and pepper. Cook for 3 minutes on Full Power. Whisk once during cooking and on removal from the cooker. Pour the sauce over the celery and heat for a further 2 minutes on Full Power.

Serve: with pork, poultry or fish dishes.

Fruit Trifle

Cooking containers : Disposable Pie Plate/Jug/Cake Dish
Cooking time : 11–14½ minutes, plus 2 hours
standing time
Number of servings : 6–8

Ingredients:
For the sponge base:
50 g/2 oz caster sugar
50 g/2 oz margarine
1 egg (size 2)
50 g/2 oz self-raising flour
50 g/2 oz mixed chopped glacé fruit
1 tablespoon hot water

For the custard:
450 ml/¾ pint milk
2 teaspoons grated lemon rind
3 tablespoons caster sugar
3 eggs (size 2)

For the filling:
1–2 glasses of sherry
411 g/14½ oz can of fruit cocktail
450 g/1 lb fresh or frozen strawberries

For the topping:
300 ml/½ pint cream, whipped
a few strawberries

Method:
Cream the sugar and margarine together. Beat in the egg; then fold in the flour, glacé fruit and hot water. Lightly grease the Pie Dish and pour in the cake mix. Cook for 3–3½ minutes on Full Power. Turn out on to a wire rack to cool.

Make the custard by heating the milk with the lemon rind in the Jug for 4 minutes or until hot. Whisk in the sugar and eggs. Cook for 4–7 minutes on Medium Power, stirring every 2 minutes until the custard thickens. Leave to cool.

Crumble the cooled cake and place in the base of the Cake Dish. Combine the sherry, fruit cocktail (including the syrup) and strawberries; then pour over the cake. When the custard is cool, pour it over the fruit. Leave for 2 hours and then cover with the whipped cream and decorate with a few strawberries.

Serve: with sponge fingers.

Variation: use different combinations of fruit or a chocolate sponge base.

Apricot and Raisin Flan ★

Cooking container	: Flan Dish
Cooking time	: 9½–10½ minutes, plus 30 minutes chilling time
Number of servings	: 5–6

Ingredients:
75 g/3 oz butter
150 g/5 oz plain flour
2 teaspoons caster sugar
1 egg yolk (size 3)
1–2 tablespoons water
350 g/12 oz cooked apricots, puréed and sweetened to taste
25 g/1 oz raisins
100 g/4 oz marzipan

Method:
Rub the butter into the flour until it resembles fine bread-crumbs. Stir in the sugar and egg yolk and bind together with water. Roll out and line the Flan Dish. Trim the edges and set the flan in the refrigerator for 30 minutes. Place a sheet of Layering Tissue in the base of the flan, cover with dried beans and cook for 3½ minutes on Full Power. Remove the Tissue and beans and cook for a further 1–2 minutes on Full Power or until the pastry is almost dry.

When the pastry case is cold, fill with the puréed fruit mixed with the raisins. Roll out the marzipan thinly and cut into thin strips. Form a lattice work of marzipan over the fruit. Heat in the cooker for 5 minutes on Full Power.

Serve: warm with cream.

Variation: use any other fruit of your choice.

Apricot and Raisin Flan

Pineapple Suet Puddings

Cooking containers : Mini Dishes
Cooking time : 5–6 minutes
Number of servings : 6

Ingredients:
3 tablespoons golden syrup
100 g/4 oz mixed glacé pineapple and angelica leaves
75 g/3 oz self-raising flour
75 g/3 oz fresh white breadcrumbs (include the crust)
75 g/3 oz shredded suet
40 g/1½ oz soft light brown sugar
1 egg (size 2)
8 tablespoons milk

Method:
Place ½ tablespoon of golden syrup into the base of each Mini
Dish. Slice some of the pineapple and place, with the angelica
leaves, in the base of each Dish. Chop up the remaining pineapple. Combine the flour, breadcrumbs, suet, sugar and chopped pineapple. Beat in the egg and milk. Divide the mixture
between the Dishes and cover loosely with Cling Film. Place
the Dishes in a circle in the cooker and cook for 5–6 minutes on
Full Power. Turn out on to serving dishes.

Serve: with custard or cream.

Hot Blackcurrant Fluff

Cooking containers : Mini Dishes/Roasting Rack Base
                     (optional)
Cooking time : 2–3 minutes
Number of servings : 6

Ingredients:
3 tablespoons sponge or fruit cake
398 g/14 oz can of blackcurrant pie filling
1 egg white (size 2)
2 tablespoons caster sugar

Method:

Crumble the cake and divide between the Mini Dishes. Cover with the pie filling. Whisk the egg white until stiff and then whisk in the caster sugar. Place the egg mixture on the top of the pie filling. Place the Mini Dishes on the Base of the Roasting Rack or on the cooker base in a circle. Cook for 2–3 minutes on Full Power until the blackcurrant is warm and the topping set.

Serve: with whipped cream. These are delicious hot or cold.

Caramel Bread Pudding ★

Cooking containers : Disposable Cake Dish/Jug
Cooking time   : 35 minutes, plus 5 minutes standing time
Number of servings : 5–6

Ingredients:

150 g/5 oz sliced bread
450 ml/¾ pint milk
80 ml/3 fl oz ginger wine
2 tablespoons water
25 g/1 oz granulated sugar
3 eggs (size 2), beaten
grated rind of 1 lemon
75 g/3 oz caster sugar
100 g/4 oz sultanas
75 g/3 oz mixed chopped glacé fruit

Method:

Cut the bread into small squares. Mix 300 ml/½ pint of the milk with the ginger wine. Pour over the bread and leave to soak. Place the water and granulated sugar in the Jug. Heat on Medium Power for approximately 10 minutes or until the mixture caramelises. Leave to cool.

Combine the eggs, 150 ml/¼ pint milk and grated lemon rind. Stir into the cold caramel. Stir in the remaining ingredients. Lightly grease the Cake Dish and pour in the mix. Cook covered for 25 minutes on Medium Power or until firm. Stand for 5 minutes and then turn the pudding out.

Serve: with cream or custard.

Entertaining

Entertaining is always a pleasure when you have a microwave cooker. Less time is spent in the kitchen and more with your guests. The dishes chosen for this section will impress not only your friends but yourself, as they are so easy to do! Most can be precooked and either heated later or served cold.

Trout with Cream ★

Cooking container : Shallow Dish
Cooking time : 14–17½ minutes
Number of servings : 4

Ingredients:
50 g/2 oz butter
25 g/1 oz breadcrumbs
25 g/1 oz chopped almonds
4 medium-size trout
1 lemon
80 ml/3 fl oz single cream
salt and pepper

Method:
Melt 25 g/1 oz butter in the Shallow Dish for 1 minute on Full Power. Stir in the breadcrumbs and almonds; then heat until crisp for 4–5 minutes on Full Power, stirring every minute. Remove from the Dish and leave to one side.

Place the trout in the Shallow Dish (head to tail). Squeeze the juice from the lemon over the fish. Dot with the remaining butter and sprinkle with seasoning. Cook covered for 8–10 minutes on Full Power or until the fish flakes.

Heat the cream until warm; 1–1½ minutes on Full Power. Pour over the trout and sprinkle with the breadcrumb mix.

Serve: garnished with lemon, with sauté or new potatoes and a green salad.

Trout with Cream

Mulligatawny Soup ★

Cooking container : Casserole Dish
Cooking time   : 55 minutes
Number of servings : 6–8

Ingredients:
1 onion
100 g/4 oz carrots
100 g/4 oz potatoes
2 small dessert apples
50 g/2 oz bacon
25 g/1 oz margarine
25 g/1 oz plain flour
1 tablespoon tomato purée
1 tablespoon garam masala
2 tablespoons mango chutney
1 teaspoon mixed dried herbs
1.5 litres/2½ pints beef stock
150 ml/¼ pint double cream
salt and pepper

Method:
Clean and prepare the onion, carrots, potatoes and apples. Chop all up finely with the bacon. Place the chopped food in the Casserole Dish and add the margarine. Cover and cook for 7 minutes on Full Power. Stir in the flour, tomato purée, garam masala, chutney and herbs. Cook covered for 3 minutes on Full Power. Gradually stir in the stock and return covered to the cooker for 45 minutes on Full Power. Purée the soup and check the seasoning; then return to the Casserole Dish. Heat as required and stir in the cream just before serving.

Serve: with crisp poppadams.

Veal Goulash ★

Cooking container   : Casserole Dish
Cooking time   : 2–2½ hours
Number of servings : 4–5

Ingredients:
900 g/2 lb stewing veal, cubed
3 onions, sliced
4 large carrots, sliced
2 tablespoons oil
2 tablespoons flour
2 tablespoons paprika
2 tablespoons tomato purée
450 ml/¾ pint chicken stock
150 ml/¼ pint beer
150 ml/¼ pint soured cream
salt and pepper

Method:
Place in the Casserole Dish the veal, onion and carrot. Sprinkle with the oil, cover and cook for 10 minutes on Full Power. Stir half-way through the cycle. Stir in the flour, paprika and tomato purée. Heat covered for 5 minutes on Full Power. Gradually stir in the stock and beer. Add seasoning. Cook covered on Full Power for 10 minutes, stir and continue cooking on Low (Defrost) Power for 1½–2 hours. (Temperature Probe setting is 90°C/190°F for 2–3 hours.) Stir in the soured cream just before serving.

Serve: with herb dumplings and sweet corn.

Crown Roast of Lamb ★

Cooking containers : Vegetable Dish/Shallow Dish
Cooking time : 23–29 minutes, plus 20 minutes
standing time
Number of servings : 6

Ingredients:

For the stuffing:
1 onion, chopped
1 tablespoon oil
225 g/8 oz sausage meat
75 g/3 oz fresh white breadcrumbs
juice and grated rind of 1 orange
2 teaspoons mixed dried herbs
100 g/4 oz sultanas
1 egg (size 3), beaten
salt and pepper

1 prepared crown roast, containing 12–14 cutlets

For the glaze:
50 g/2 oz dark soft brown sugar
2 tablespoons orange juice
1 tablespoon Worcestershire sauce
25 g/1 oz butter

Method:

Cook the onion with the oil in the Vegetable Dish, covered, for 3 minutes on Full Power. Stir in all the stuffing ingredients, binding together with the egg. Place the crown roast on the Shallow Dish and fill the centre with the stuffing. Combine together the sugar, juice and Worcestershire sauce and brush this over the stuffing and outside of the crown. Dot with the butter. Cook on Full Power until the internal temperature of the meat reaches 75°C/170°F, approximately 20–26 minutes. (Place your Probe or thermometer through 3–4 cutlets, entering where a join is made.) Brush with the glaze during cooking. Wrap with foil on removal from the cooker and stand for 20 minutes before serving.

Crown Roast of Lamb

Chicken Liver Pâté ★

Cooking containers : Shallow Dish/Mini Dishes
Cooking time : 13–15 minutes
Number of servings : 6

Ingredients:
1 onion, chopped
1 clove of garlic, crushed
25 g/1 oz butter
350 g/12 oz chicken livers, prepared
4 tablespoons double cream
1 tablespoon brown sherry
salt and pepper

Method:
Place the onion, garlic and butter in the Shallow Dish and cook covered for 3 minutes on Full Power. Stir in the chicken livers and cook covered on Medium Power for 10–12 minutes or until the livers are still just pink inside. Allow to cool; then blend or purée with the cream, sherry, salt and pepper. Turn the mixture into the Mini Dishes and chill before serving.

Serve: garnished with parsley or a sliced olive, on Melba toast or french bread.

Broccoli-stuffed Tomatoes

Cooking containers : Jug/Mini Dishes
Cooking time : 12–16 minutes
Number of servings : 6

Ingredients:
6 tomatoes (to fit in the Mini Dishes)
175 g/6 oz broccoli, cooked
2 rashers of bacon, chopped
1 small onion, chopped finely
40 g/1½ oz cheese, grated
salt and pepper

Method:
Slice the tops off the tomatoes, scoop out the flesh and chop the flesh and tops up roughly. Chop the broccoli. Cook the bacon

Index

Citrus Cheesecake ★

Cooking container : Flan Dish
Cooking time : 13–15 minutes
Number of servings : 5–6

Ingredients:
25 g/1 oz butter
25 g/1 oz caster sugar
150 g/5 oz ginger biscuits, crushed
225 g/8 oz cottage cheese
225 g/8 oz cream cheese
50 g/2 oz caster sugar
3 eggs (size 2)
grated rind of 1 lemon
1 tablespoon lemon juice
150 ml/¼ pint double cream

Method:
Melt the butter for 1 minute on Full Power in the Flan Dish; then stir in the sugar and crushed ginger nuts. Press down firmly into the base of the Dish. Sieve the cottage cheese and mix with the cream cheese, caster sugar, eggs, lemon rind and juice. Pour on to the biscuit base. Cook on Full Power for 2 minutes and then Low Power for 10–12 minutes or until set. Leave to cool, whip the cream and spread some over the cheesecake, piping the remaining cream around the edge.

Serve: sprinkled with lemon peel: cook strips of peel in 50 ml/2 fl oz water with 50 g/2 oz caster sugar until syrupy (approximately 6–7 minutes on Full Power) and arrange them on the cheesecake.

Variation: serve topped with any fruit of your choice.